How Food Is Made

Level 9 – Gold

Helpful Hints for Reading at Home

The graphemes (written letters) and phonemes (units of sound) used throughout this series are aligned with Letters and Sounds. This offers a consistent approach to learning whether reading at home or in the classroom.

HERE ARE SOME COMMON WORDS THAT YOUR CHILD MIGHT FIND TRICKY:

water	where	would	know	thought	through	couldn't
laughed	eyes	once	we're	school	can't	our

TOP TIPS FOR HELPING YOUR CHILD TO READ:

- Encourage your child to read aloud as well as silently to themselves.
- Allow your child time to absorb the text and make comments.
- Ask simple questions about the text to assess understanding.
- Encourage your child to clarify the meaning of new vocabulary.

This book focuses on developing independence, fluency and comprehension. It is a Gold level 9 book band.

©2023 **BookLife Publishing Ltd.**
King's Lynn, Norfolk PE30 4LS, UK

ISBN 978-1-80505-056-8

All rights reserved. Printed in China.
A catalogue record for this book is available from the British Library.

How Food Is Made
Written by Harriet Brundle and Shalini Vallepur
Adapted by Rebecca Phillips-Bartlett
Designed by Jasmine Pointer

FSC
www.fsc.org
MIX
Paper from responsible sources
FSC® C113515

Image Credits Images are courtesy of Shutterstock.com. With thanks to Getty Images, Thinkstock Photo and iStockphoto. Cover – Wise ant, Natalia89, Elena.D. 4–5 – Elena Elisseeva, forden. 6–7 – Dan Su Sa, LilKar. 8–9 – Juice Flair, msheldrake, Yoyochow23. 10–11 – HandmadePictures, Ljupco Smokovski, M. Unal Ozmen, Chones, casanisa. 12–13 – Zigzag Mountain Art, J_K. 14–15 – Yatra4289, Bits And Splits, Matyas Rehak. 16–17 – Alter-ego, Ixepop. 18–19 – saiko3p, Volosina, photowind. 20–21 – ilkka Kukko, Lesya_boyko.

Contents

Page 4   From Field to Feast

Page 6   The Path to Potatoes

Page 10   The Beginning of Bread

Page 14   The Story of Sugar

Page 18   The Course of Chocolate

Page 22   Index

Page 23   Questions

From Field to Feast

Our food does not just appear on our plates. Instead, it has to be made. Lots of our food starts its journey as a plant in a field.

Plants that are used for food are called crops.

There are some plants that we eat just as they grow, but other foods go through many steps to turn them into food. We are going to learn how some different foods turn from crops into foods that we eat.

The Path to Potatoes

From mash potato to French fries, potatoes can be used in many different ways. Whichever potato is your favourite, they all start in the same way. Potatoes are grown in the ground. First, a seed potato is planted.

Seed potato

Above the ground, potato plants grow leaves, but the new potatoes are hidden underground. Farmers use the leaves to know when the potatoes are ready. When the leaves turn yellow that means it is time to dig up the potatoes.

Some potatoes are sold at farmers' markets. Other potatoes are sent to factories to be cleaned and packaged ready to be sold in shops. Some potatoes will be sent to different factories where they are used to make something else.

Potatoes can be made into many different foods. From hash browns to packets of crisps, they all come from potatoes. There are plenty of ways to cook fresh potatoes too, such as baking, roasting or boiling them.

Hash browns

The Beginning of Bread

Bread is eaten all over the world. It can come in many different shapes and sizes. While it can look and taste very different, most bread is made using the same basic ingredients. These are flour, water, yeast and salt.

First, these ingredients are mixed together and made into a stretchy ball of dough. This dough is pressed, folded and stretched. This is called kneading. After it has been kneaded, the bread is left to rest. This helps it rise.

Bread dough can be cooked in lots of different ways. The way it is cooked depends on the type of bread that is being made. Bagels are boiled in water before being baked in an oven.

Some bakers add other ingredients to their bread, such as fruits, cheese and olives. Bread can be made into different shapes, such as baguettes or rolls. Bread dough can even be made to use in other foods, such as pizzas.

The Story of Sugar

Sugar is grown on farms in lots of different countries around the world. We get sugar from two plants called sugarcane and sugar beet. They are very different plants, but the sugar inside is exactly the same.

Sugarcane

Sugar beet

To turn sugar beet and sugarcane into sugar they go to a factory. Here, they are cut into tiny pieces. These pieces are crushed until they make a sugary juice. The juice is boiled which turns it into syrup.

As the syrup cools down, tiny sugar crystals form. These crystals are cleaned and packaged and sold in shops as sugar! It is thought that people have been using sugar for around 10,000 years. It has many different uses.

Some sugar is sold in shops and people use it to bake cakes and biscuits. Other sugar is turned into something else before it is sold in shops. Some sugar is boiled and stretched into shapes to make sweets.

The Course of Chocolate

Chocolate is made from cocoa beans. These beans are found inside cocoa pods which grow on trees. Once they have been taken out of the pods, the beans are dried by a machine or the sun.

Cocoa pods

Cocoa beans

Once the beans are dried, they go to a factory. There, the beans are cleaned and roasted to bring out the delicious chocolate flavour. The beans are ground up which turns them into a thick brown liquid called cocoa mass.

Once the cocoa mass has been made, other ingredients might be added. Other ingredients might include milk, fruit or nuts. This mixture is put into another machine which makes it smooth. The liquid chocolate is poured into moulds.

The chocolate is cooled down so that it sets and becomes solid. The chocolate is put into its packaging and sent away to be sold. You can buy many different types of chocolate, such as milk chocolate and dark chocolate.

Index

bagels 12
cocoa beans 18–20
crystals 16
hash browns 9
leaves 7

How to Use an Index

An index helps us to find information in a book. Each word has a set of page numbers. These page numbers are where you can find information about that word.

Page numbers

Example: balloons 5, <u>8–10</u>, 19

Important word

This means page 8, page 10, and all the pages in between. Here, it means pages 8, 9 and 10.

Questions

1. How do farmers know when it is time to dig up potatoes?

2. What are the two plants that we use to make sugar?

3. What other ingredients might people add to chocolate?

4. Use the contents page to find out about the beginning of bread.

5. Use the index page to find hash browns in this book.